A Woman's ABC's Of Life

LESSONS IN LOVE, FAMILY, AND CAREER FROM THOSE WHO LEARNED THE HARD WAY

BECA LEWIS

Perception Publishing

All rights reserved. No part of this book may be reproduced or transmitted in any form or by any means, electronic or mechanical, including photocopying, recording, or by any information storage and retrieval system, without written permission from the author, except for the inclusion of brief quotations in a review.

Copyright ©1994 Beca Lewis

ISBN: 978-0-9719529-4-2

All rights reserved. No part of this book may be reproduced or transmitted in any form or by any means, electronic or mechanical, including photocopying, recording, or by any information storage and retrieval system, without written permission from the author, except for the inclusion of brief quotations in a review.

Copyright ©1994 Beca Lewis

Contents

Dedication — VII

The ABC's Of Romantic Love — 1
Part One

1. How To Recognize And Keep A Good Man — 3

2. Being A Wife — 9

3. Being An Ex-Wife — 15

4. Pleasing A Man — 21

The ABC's Of A Career — 27
Part Two

5. Being A Student — 29

6. Going On A Job Interview — 35

7. On The Job	41
8. Owning Your Own Business	47
The ABC's of Family Relationships Part Three	53
9. Dealing With Parents	55
10. Being A Mother	61
11. Being A Stepmother	67
12. Being A Grandmother	73
The ABC's of Living Part Four	79
13. Staying Healthy	81
14. As Time Passes	87
15. Personal Pleasures	93
16. Life In General	99
Author's Notes	105
Also By Beca	107
About Beca	109

Dedication

This book began with a request from my youngest daughter. She often called me from college to ask advice for her and her friends. Finally, she asked me to write it all down, and voila! A book was born. My advice at that time for young women. And since many of their questions began with dating and love, I started there.

Most of this advice grew out of observations from my own life. Though it was often filled with soap-opera-type plots, I discovered that in the end, it is not the ride that counts; it's what you walk away with.

I have walked away with a heart filled with gratitude for my children, who took the ride with me, and my friends, who were there to support me. Thanks to all of you, but specifically those who helped make this book a reality:

To my parents, Arthur and Celeste Lewis, who must have found it difficult to have a daughter who questioned everything, and yet believed in the impossible.

To my sister, Jamie Lewis, who by looking up to me, gave me a reason for living up to an ideal.

To my children: Charles Wareham, Christin Von Musser, and Laurie Lewis-Knoedler, for loving me through it all.

To my mentor, Dorothy Hardy, for all that you taught me.

To my husband, Delbert Lee Piper Sr., who supports and inspires me.

To what I have learned: To not indulge in what is not good, but rejoice in all that is.

The ABC's Of Romantic Love

Part One

ONE

How To Recognize And Keep A Good Man

Acknowledge your man often as possible. Tell him how wonderful he is to you. Pick something good about him to focus on, no matter how small. He has to start somewhere.

Beware of a man who is just getting over another serious relationship.

Count out a man who is abusive physically, verbally, or emotionally. In this case, the words "I love you" are abusive too. Leave.

Discover your man's values and honor them as if they were your own.

Enjoy your life when he's not around. He loved you for the life you had before you met, so don't stop now!

Forget a "Mommy's boy."

HOW TO RECOGNIZE AND KEEP A GOOD MAN

Give up a man who spends all his spare time "hanging with the boys." He will not grow out of it just because you came into his life.

Hold on to a man who knows that behind every good man there is a good woman—and he loves it!

Involve your man in your life. He needs to know he is valuable to you.

Justify his trust in you. Never betray him in thought, word, or action.

Keep a man who knows that behind every good woman there is a good man, and he is willing to be that man for you.

L et him do what he does best and you do what you do best. Be equal partners.

M ake sure you realize that once you sleep with a man, you have lost your ability to think objectively.

N ever give a man an ultimatum. You will lose! Give him enough valid reasons to do what you want, and he will. Don't tell him, show him.

O bserve his actions. They speak louder than words. Observe your actions. Make sure they match what you say.

P arenthood is an important issue. Be sure your man shares your views on this subject.

HOW TO RECOGNIZE AND KEEP A GOOD MAN

Qualify a man's intention. Remember, many of them have one goal, sex.

Run from a man who has been to hell and has decided to wallow in the experience. That's all he will ever be able to do. He won't be able to make a commitment to his own progress in life, let alone yours.

Split from a man who thinks everything is everyone else's fault, especially yours.

Treasure a man who has been to hell and came back.

Understand that a man may always "look."

Value the time a man spends with you. Time is his greatest gift, so don't waste it by whining about what he does wrong.

❧

Want a man who has learned how to put his relationship with you first.

❧

X-rate your past love life. This is for only you to remember. Just tell him he is the best (and make it true).

❧

Yearn to understand first and to be understood second.

❧

Zero in on a man who loves to love you well.

Two

Being A Wife

Ask about all joint finances. Become part of the decision process. If you are the one in charge of finances, make sure your husband is included in the decision process.

Be careful not to turn the words "husband" and "wife" into job descriptions.

Create a home environment that will make him love to come home.

Don't fence yourself or him in.

Establish credit in your own name, not just as a tag-on to your husband's account.

Find someone you can completely trust to talk to if your marriage is not working.

Grow wiser together.

Have a savings account in your name. Save consistently.

If a fight occurs, never bring up old issues, and never call him names or label him.

Jokes made at each other's expense are not funny.

Keep intimacies and secrets sacred. They should stay only between the two of you.

Learn about what interests him most so you can talk about it intelligently.

Make a wonderful marriage a priority. It will be a strong and consistent base for everything else that either of you do.

Never blame each other for anything. State the problem and find a way to solve it together.

Open your heart.

Plan exciting things to do together, each week, month, year, and far into the future.

Quietly and consistently view your husband as the most wonderful man in the world. Treat him as such, and watch what happens!

Refrain from including your best friend in everything you and your husband plan.

Set a weekly "date" night, and keep it.

The only way to keep your man is to give him freedom to be himself.

United you stand, divided you fall. Heal all divisions immediately. Keep an eye out for the small and subtle ones, as they are the most dangerous.

Veto any thought of withholding sex as punishment, or using it as a reward.

Withdrawing in any way is a slow and certain death to a relationship. Keep communicating!

X & O's. Your kisses and hugs may not be acknowledged at first, but they are seeds in a garden. Eventually, they will produce flowers.

※

You may spend hours on the phone with your girlfriends when your husband is not home. When he is home, make him your priority, so he can make you his.

※

Zap the belief that once you are married, you don't have to look good. Become more beautiful, both inside and out, with each passing year.

Three

Being An Ex-Wife

A nalyze what you did wrong the first time and don't do it again in your next relationship.

※

B e careful when dating a new man. If he is nice to you, you might think this is love

※

C ultivate interests you kept on hold while you were married.

※

Drop all comparisons between your ex-husband and your new love.

❦

Explain to your children, in a way that they can understand, everything that is going on. Don't keep it a secret. They will know something is happening and will invent their own scenarios.

❦

Forgive your ex-husband for what he did wrong. Not forgiving keeps the pattern in your life and it will show up again with someone else.

❦

Get excited about what the future offers.

❦

Hanging onto "what ifs" keeps you chained to the past. The key is self-forgiveness. That was then, this is now.

If you are still in his life, be a true friend to his new wife.

Join a support group.

Keep your friends. These are the people who love and support you no matter what man is in your life.

Let him go.

Make sure that your children are very clear that they are not the cause of the divorce.

Negotiate terms in your divorce that do not make you a victim now, or in the future.

Organize your assets. Be sure to transfer them to your name.

Practice safe sex.

Qualify new men in your life carefully. It may be wise to have them investigated before starting a serious relationship.

Redecorate your old home, or decorate your new one, to reflect your personal style. This time you don't need to make any compromises.

S ay nice things about your ex-husband to your children. They need a father they can look up to.

T ake time to know yourself.

⋖⋗

U nderstand clearly what you want next time, and don't settle for less. Choose qualities in a man that match your values.

⋖⋗

V italize your look! Remember, the best revenge is looking good.

⋖⋗

W hen he remarries, don't interfere.

X-husbands are a learning experience, not a life sentence.

You are wiser than you were before. Treasure that wisdom, and use it.

Zillions of accusations will never make the past right. Leave the past out of any current discussions you have with your ex-husband.

Four

Pleasing A Man

Asking if he loves you is telling him that he has failed at showing you. Actions do speak louder than words. Appreciate what he does.

※

Be aware that one of his greatest fears may be that if he loves you, he will lose himself. Help him see that loving you means he can be more of himself.

※

Clutching, begging, and being moody are three sure ways to lose a man. Not to mention your self-respect.

Discuss what is important to you when your emotion over the issue has faded into the background.

Everyone wants to be allowed to be happy. Men are no different.

Feeding a man is the way to his heart. But, you don't have to cook the meal.

Give clear indications about sex. Men sometimes can't tell.

Honor him and your relationship.

If you feel you must say it, don't! Not then. Wait until the emotions fade.

Just saying, "Oh, nothing," when he asks what's bothering you, could be interpreted as a rejection. Tell him as much of the truth as you can.

Keep negative thoughts to yourself.

Let him do things for you, and be grateful!

Men are simple to understand. They just want to know you will always let them be men.

Nothing pleases a man more than knowing you want to please him.

Okay, sometimes he wants you to wear cute clothes. Wear them and enjoy his attention.

Physical actions, like washing your car, are often his way of saying, "I love you!"

Quell your desire to be a "know it all," even if you do. Keep quiet and let him find it out for himself.

Realize that a man doesn't like to be rejected and often will not make the first move. Make it clear that if he asks, you won't say "no."

Surprise him with small, useful gifts. Even if he says he doesn't like surprises he'll love this kind—and you.

Take him to places he has never been before. Plan everything yourself so he can feel pampered.

Understand that very few men want to marry a woman who has slept around a lot, but they do want a woman who is unafraid to love.

Verbalize your love.

Want to discuss something important? Take him out to eat.

X-ray your motives before you do anything that may jeopardize the relationship.

Yield when necessary and safe your you.

Zing him with your happiness because he is around.

The ABC's Of A Career

Part Two

Five

Being A Student

Attend your graduation and buy a school ring.

Break bad habits now, before you accept them as part of your character.

Call your parents.

D iscover the value and joys of the library.

E njoy every minute of school. It will be a time you will remember with pleasure for the rest of your life.

F ind a self-defense class and take it.

G et your new friends' addresses when you leave school. Keep in touch.

H elp new students get acquainted. Introduce them to your favorite places and people.

Ignore anyone who says you can't. If it is something you are impelled to do, find a way and do it.

Join a school organization.

Keep the current catalog of your school's classes. You will need the course descriptions later if you go back to school or transfer.

Label your clothes so they don't get mixed up in your roommate's laundry.

Make the acquaintance of the Dean of your college.

N ominate yourself to something that brings out your talents.

O wn a Swiss army knife with lots of attachments and keep it with you.

P lan your school career with the help of a guidance counselor.

Q uiz yourself as you study.

R emember, the purpose of school is to get an education and to learn to think.

S tay in school for your own good!

T ake a variety of courses. In the process, you might find your life's passion.

U nderstand how the system works, and make it work for you.

V iew good study habits as money in the bank and free time in your life. Learn them and use them.

W atch your eating habits. Start eating healthy now. You'll learn more, look better and live longer.

Xerox copies of all your school records. You'll need them again someday.

⋆

Yes, you can—and should—ask for help from your teachers when you need it.

⋆

Zone out occasionally. Take a break to take care of your emotional needs.

Six

Going On A Job Interview

Absorb everything asked of you and practice your responses for the next interview.

Bring a resume that is tailored to the job for which you are interviewing. Get help in writing the perfect resume

Comment on something that interests you about the interviewer or the items in his or her office.

Don't bring up anything unflattering about your past unless you are asked about it.

Echo the interview questions by rephrasing them before you answer.

Forget wearing perfume that day. Your interviewer may be allergic to it, or it may remind them of someone.

Give several reasons why hiring you will produce the results the company wants.

Habitually send "thank you" letters as soon as possible after the interview.

I nitial impressions are hard to overcome. Make yours outstanding!

J uggling a briefcase and a purse can be difficult. Try carrying just a briefcase.

K now your strong areas and promote them. If you are asked about your weaknesses, show how you are overcoming them or turning them into assets.

L et them know clearly what you can do for them. Remember, you are unique.

M entally review possible questions and the answers you will give.

Never, never be late!

On corporate interviews, take the conservative approach with dress, hair, and makeup.

Practice your handshake. A firm handshake conveys confidence and competence.

Question the interviewer regarding how he or she envisions your role in the company, then explain how you can fulfill that vision.

Research the company before you go on the interview.

GOING ON A JOB INTERVIEW

Scope out how people dress at the company and dress that way, top of the line.

Try on your new outfit before you go so you will look and feel comfortable.

Upgrade the image you have of yourself. If asked if you can perform a certain task, even if you are uncertain, say "yes." Take a class or get help so you can.

Volunteer information only about your work performance. Keep your personal life to yourself.

Wear your best clothes. It will help your morale.

X-out the loud or chunky jewelry.

You can make a great impression with a company by impressing the receptionist first with your sincerity and professionalism.

Zip through a typing or computer skills test by practicing before you go on the interview.

Seven

On The Job

Always write down the name of the person on the other end of the telephone line. You may later need to verify the information they gave you.

※

Break down tasks and do them one step at a time, priority steps first.

※

Cut out the time you hang out at other people's desks.

D̶o the job the way they ask you to do it, and do it well. After that, you can show them a better way.

E̶arn the respect of your coworkers and boss by being efficient.

F̶ind a way to enjoy every job you do. In order for things to change, you must be grateful for what you have.

G̶ossiping will label you as "one of the girls."

H̶ave a sense of urgency when working on a project.

Improve your value by taking outside classes.

Jump at the chance to do a project that looks too hard.

Keep a jug of good water at your desk. It will keep your desire for coffee and munchies at bay.

Look for a mentor and gratefully learn all you can from that person.

Motivate your staff by first finding out what motivates them.

Never have an office romance with the boss. If you must, find a new boss first.

Offer to do what you know how to do. Otherwise, your talents might go unnoticed.

Pretend this is your own business. It might be someday.

Question everybody about their jobs and how each one fits into the whole picture.

Resolve to not believe anything you hear about co-workers unless they have told you themselves.

Study all advances in your field.

❧

Take time to evaluate if your job is moving you toward your long-term goals, and what you can do to improve the situation if necessary.

❧

Undertake the task of writing a manual for your position. This will make it easier to train someone to take your place so that you can move up in the company.

❧

Valuable information can be learned by being the person who is listening, not talking.

❧

Write down the skills that you learn and file them. This may help jog your memory when you write your next resume or a proposal for a raise.

X-hibit a cooperative attitude at all times. When you can no longer approach your job with enthusiasm, perhaps it's time to find a new job.

You can plan for future opportunities by networking with people at other companies who work in your field.

Zip your lip before you give personal information to co-workers. You never know how it might come back to haunt you.

Eight

Owning Your Own Business

Always do "tasks for cash" first in the business day.

Be an expert at what you do.

Create relationships. This in turn will create a business.

Determine if you want to create a market or cater to an existing one. This one decision will affect what kind of business you choose.

Educate yourself as to how big businesses and markets work. Use the information to your advantage.

Find a way to take time off. Your business doesn't own you, you own it, remember?

Get expert advice, and take it.

Hire people who know things you don't know, and can do their job better than you. Then help them do it.

nventory your values and make sure your business is in harmony with them. Otherwise, if you succeed, it will be at the expense of everything you believe in.

oin and become active in organizations that support women and your business.

eep the vision of why you are in business at the forefront of all business decisions.

ove doing what you love to do.

ake your reputation synonymous with your business.

Negotiate all your deals from the point of view that everyone must benefit.

Offer to write articles about your field of expertise. This is a great way to become known as an expert. If you don't write well, find someone who does, and collaborate.

Put together a sound marketing plan and evaluate its performance monthly.

Quietly build a network of people that can provide you information, or help, at a moment's notice.

Return calls as soon as possible. Callers may be in the minor leagues today, but tomorrow could become a major league player one with a long memory!

Sell when you are at the top.

Tell your clients how your product or service can help them, and then give them even more than you promised.

Understand that the best way to inspire your staff is to stay inspired yourself.

Value yourself, your talents, and your time. If you don't, then no one else will either.

Wear the best shoes you can afford. Many people judge your status based on your shoes and how you take care of them.

X-out any client that undermines you or your business.

You are promoting your business in everything you say, wear, or do. Make sure it is always excellent.

Zealously pay attention to details.

The ABC's of Family Relationships

Part Three

Nine

Dealing With Parents

Acknowledge their contribution to your life.

Breakaway if necessary.

Communicate anything that has been bothering you so that it can be resolved if possible.

Develop your own self-image. You are not just your parents' child.

Evaluate what you learned from them, then decide what is useful and what is not.

Forgive them for what they did or did not do. This way, you can get on with your life.

Get your mother or father to write down the recipes for your favorite dishes.

Help them plan for their future. If their future is not carefully planned, it may become yours.

Investigate your heritage.

Joyfully hug them hello and goodbye.

Keep them up-to-date with what your children are doing. Allow them to be important in your children's lives.

Let them know what you love—or like—about them.

Make an effort to get to know them. Find out what their lives are like when they aren't being parents.

Next time you visit, hide a present for them. One day when you would like to be there but can't, you can tell them where to find it.

Often parents really know what they are talking about. Listen to what they mean and don't debate the words; you may hear their wisdom.

Parents are people, just like you. The day you really understand this, you have grown up.

Question your parents about their childhood. Record or video the discussion.

Realize that a mother's or father's love can, and often does, come from people other than your parents.

Share your hopes and dreams with them. It's possible that they will help you achieve them.

Take videos of your family throughout the year. Make it your Holiday present to your parents each year.

Unearth their secret dream and help them accomplish it.

Verify what you remember from your childhood by asking them now, while you still can.

Write down what you would do differently as a parent, then do it. If it doesn't work, you can always do what they did.

X-out the need to make your parents proud of you. Be proud of yourself.

You will enjoy your parents more when you give up how you wish they had been, and instead, see them for what they are and be grateful for it.

Zealously send cards, notes, and letters, especially on special occasions.

Ten

Being A Mother

A well-rounded child is a happy child and will become a happy adult.

B e prepared to grow up yourself.

C reate traditions. In times of great change, these are the things that children can count on.

Demonstrate to your children what love looks like, so they have a model on how to love others.

Educate your children to love education. Reading to them is a great first step. Turn off the TV and provide lots of books.

Find a way to give clear guidelines as to what is expected of them.

Give your children reasons to do well. Physical punishment is not a good reason. Logical explanation helps them make good decisions when you are not there for them to fear.

Help your children discover what is special about them.

⋆

In no time at all, your children will be grown. Make time for them now!

⋆

Just remember: How you let your sons treat you when they're young will be exactly how they treat other women when they grow up.

⋆

Keep your word or explain logically why you can not.

⋆

Listen to your children before you jump to conclusions. They may be right.

⋆

Making your adult children choose between you and their spouse will never make you happy.

Notice good behavior and reward it. Give bad behavior a quick reprimand, but do not dwell on it. All they want is attention. Give it to them for the right reasons.

Once you are a mother, always be a mother first.

Put "happy notes" into their lunch box.

Quietly and gently guide. Lead by example.

Remember, you have until they are three years old to teach them what love feels like, and until age five to teach them their own value and the value of others. If they have learned these two things by then, they will have a solid foundation.

Sew visible hearts onto the backs of their clothes so they can tell front from back, and at the same time be reminded you love them.

The greatest gifts you can give a child are guidelines for behavior and the ability to be independent.

Underline the necessity for them to assist anyone who is less fortunate.

Value their desire to be independent. Setting them free is the only way to keep them.

Write a yearly letter to each child. Save the letters until your child's 18th birthday, and present them as a collection.

X-out any negative statements to or about your children.

Your children can not live the life you wish you would have had. They are here to live their own, so help them.

Zero in on what makes them happy, and find a way to help them achieve it.

Eleven

Being A Stepmother

A ct as if you belong there. You do.

B e equal in the treatment of your children and his.

C ompliment your husband on his children.

Don't make your spouse choose between you and his children. You will lose, whichever choice he makes.

Establish a daily routine that everyone can count on.

Find a way to have quiet time with your husband with no children around.

Give them an opportunity to go to a camp each summer so they have time to develop, away from family expectations.

Help their mother stay in touch. Send her pictures and schoolwork. Remember, it's what you would want if the situation were reversed.

It's true that you can not, and should, not take the place of their mother, but you are their parent. Step up to the plate and be one.

Look for everything wonderful in your stepchildren, then tell them what you find.

Make a point of listening and understanding your stepchildren. Then, you can ask them to understand you.

Notice what doesn't work and correct it immediately.

Obtain medical permission from their mother in case of an emergency.

Plan family outings in which everyone can participate.

Quench any desire to tell your stepchildren in anger, "You're just like your mother."

Respect your husband's wishes regarding his children. If you don't agree with him, discuss it out of the sight and hearing of the children.

Stay true to who you are, so your stepchildren can get to know and love the real you.

Take the time to attend school events and visit their teachers. Let them know you care about their lives and their future.

U nderstand that your stepchildren may be slow to demonstrate their love for you. Decide that it's unimportant, and just love them.

V erify any messages sent through the children from their mother.

W hat makes you a parent is choosing to act like one.

X mas and other holidays should not be a time when children must choose between those they love. Make it easy for them. If necessary, celebrate your holidays on a different day.

Y ou must be sure you are willing to be a stepparent before your marriage.

Zigzag your way through the minefields of step-parenting with grace. Your reward will be the knowledge of a job well done, and the gratitude and respect of your husband.

Twelve

Being A Grandmother

A llow yourself to become a legend to your grandchildren. Be someone they can tell all their friends about.

B e your grandchild's best friend.

C elebrate that you are a grandparent. What a gift!

D elight in the fact that the best part of your life is now.

E ncourage all your grandchildren's dreams and be their advocate.

F ind a way to be with them for the holidays if possible.

G ive gifts to your children on their children's birthdays.

H onor your grandchildren's individuality.

Interfere in the raising of your grandchildren only when their mental or physical safety is in jeopardy.

Juggle your life so you can be with your daughter when your grandchildren are born.

Know that being a grandmother is a state of mind, not an age.

Let your children know how well they are doing with their children, and how proud you are of them.

Make up for what you couldn't do for your children by helping them now with theirs.

Never betray your grandchildren's trust. When they tell you a secret, keep it a secret.

Offer your grandchildren what they need most: someone who will listen to them.

Put away money for your grandchildren's futures.

Quench your grandchildren's desire to know more about their parents by telling positive anecdotes about their parents when they were young.

Repair any breaches in communication as quickly as possible.

Support the guidelines your children have set for their children. If you must disagree, do it in private.

Take them places they would never be able to go on their own.

Undertake the task of putting your estate in order.

Videotape yourself telling the family history. Give copies to your children and grandchildren.

Welcome the fact you once again have "children" in your life, now that you know so much more about how to enjoy them.

X marks the spot where your treasure lies in your family. Share your wisdom and love with them every chance you get.

Yummy treats are always grandmother territory.

Zoom to their rescue when they need you.

The ABC's of Living

Part Four

Thirteen

Staying Healthy

Always think about health first. Without it, nothing else is the same.

Be creative about exercise. It doesn't need to look like it does on television.

Cutting out any one of the three components to exercise—aerobic, weight resistance, and stretching—is like having a three-legged stool with two legs.

D ining out is a pleasure, not an excuse.

E njoy what you eat, not eat to enjoy.

F ind your own way of eating that keeps you healthy, and stick with it.

G ravity has a harder time affecting toned muscles.

H ave a partner in health. The goal is to encourage each other to do better and not to agree with each other's excuses.

It's ridiculous to work hard to become rich but ignore your body to the point you don't like the way you look. Money can't buy self-esteem any more than it can buy health or love.

Joints get stronger when you require them to work.

Keeping old habits narrows your options. Get rid of them and be free to make new choices.

Listen to your body. If you haven't heard it for a while, it may take some practice.

Mental health and physical health can not be separated.

Never eat a heavy meal within two hours of going to bed.

Overeating, smoking, and drinking are health thieves. Don't give up the wealth of your health for these short-term satisfactions.

Push away your plate before you finish your meal. Which is cheaper? Wasting food or paying to get it off your body?

Quickly take care of any health problems. Putting them off does not make them go away.

Resolve always to take care of your health first.

Snacking isn't bad, it's what and how much you snack on, and when and why.

Trying to control desires only makes them stronger. Observe and disown them, without judgment or guilt, and they will dissolve.

Unkind words to yourself about your body only make the problem worse. Learn to love your body! As soon as you love it, you will take better care of it.

Verify all advertising claims before you fall for a new health fad. Someone wants you to buy into it because they make money when you do.

When you get older you need less food. Accept it and eat less. Think of it this way: Now you have more money to spend elsewhere!

X-out the habit of rewarding yourself with food. Pick a more productive reward.

You have only so many calories per day to spend. Determine your calorie "budget" and spend it wisely.

Zesty thinking produces zesty living.

Fourteen

As Time Passes

As friends and family become older and wish to pass on, respect and honor their wishes, and let them go when it's time.

❧

Be flexible.

❧

Check to be sure that the life and health insurance policies for you and your spouse are adequate for yours and your loved ones needs.

Decide not to count birthdays. Want to celebrate a special day? Count trips around the sun.

Exercise is not an option. It is a necessity.

Find something new to learn and become an expert at it.

Getting older is not an excuse for anything.

Hang out with young people. Feeling young is a state of mind, not an age.

I gnite a fire in your best friend and do something exciting together.

J ealously guard your time. Don't waste it on unimportant things.

K eeping the pains and regrets of the past is the primary cause of aging. Rewrite the past or forget it.

L earn to love the good in everyone and everything, but most of all yourself.

M ake the most of every moment of every day.

Notice that you feel old only when you notice that other people are getting older. Stop looking at age.

Occasionally update your image to keep up with the times.

Plan pleasures and trips for many years in the future.

Quit talking about old age and its problems. You will just make more of them.

Realize that you, as a woman, might live longer than your mate. Plan together for your welfare and you will be able to remember him in peace and with love.

Saying "No, I can't" will age you faster than the years. Saying "Yes, I can" will turn back the clock.

There are many physical problems associated with aging that can be avoided. Stay fit, so you'll head them off before they can take root.

Understand that advertisers make money selling you the idea of old age and the products you'll need. You don't have to play along.

Variety is the spice of life. Pick one new thing to do each week, or change the way you do something now.

Wisdom: Use it, don't collect it.

X-tra attention should be paid to all the friends that you have collected through the years. If you don't know where they are, find them.

Youth is only wasted on the young if you don't claim it for yourself.

Zoom in on all the desires that you have put on hold, and do them.

Fifteen

Personal Pleasures

A llow yourself to hire someone to clean your home.

B uy flowers for yourself.

C ultivate a garden or house plants.

Dance! Dance at home, go out to dance or take a dance class. It works like magic.

Eat your favorite food often!

Find a wonderful masseuse and get a body massage.

Get a great haircut, one that expresses who you really are.

Hot water, bubbles, and candlelight will restore your peace.

Imagine yourself in your favorite sanctuary, whether real or imaginary.

Jump at the chance to go shopping. Buy something special for someone you love.

Kick your shoes off and get a foot massage.

Light a fire and cuddle up by it.

Manicures and pedicures are an inexpensive way to feel like a million bucks.

Nourish your mind by attending a play, class, or lecture. They will broaden your perspective.

Occasionally sit in a steam room, sauna or Jacuzzi.

Purchase something, no matter how small, that reminds you how wonderful you are.

Question everything you don't understand, and even some things you do.

Read a good book.

Stroll through the woods, a garden, or an open-air market.

Take naps.

Update your clothes with new accessories.

Volunteer for a charity or political cause.

Write a list of everything you do that makes you happy. Next time you're depressed, pick something off the list, and do it!

X-out time in your datebook to spend only on yourself.

Yoga is great for the body, mind, and spirit. Try a class for a great stress reducer.

Zip down to the nearest makeup artist and get a makeover.

Sixteen

Life In General

A llow more time than you think you need for everything!

B e kinder than you think is necessary.

C reate learning and growing opportunities for yourself.

Dry clean all pieces of an outfit at the same time, even if you didn't wear each piece. Dry cleaning solutions vary and may alter the color of the fabric.

Expect miracles to happen all the time. Find the good in everything.

Feel grateful for everything you have. It will open doors to more.

Go with your gut feeling, especially if it conflicts with the message you're hearing.

Have a good attorney as a personal friend.

Introduce yourself by stating your first and last name. This is much more powerful than your first name alone.

Joyfully live each moment of the day.

Keep a memory box.

Let someone know where you are at all times, for safety's sake.

Make your physical and financial health your number one priorities. Learn how to take care of your body and your investments.

Now is the time to do the things you have dreamed about. There may not be a tomorrow to do them.

Once in a while, be outrageous!

Put everything into perspective and keep your priorities straight.

Quickly pay off all your debt. Don't use debt for anything that doesn't produce a return.

Research and practice the customs of any country you are planning to visit.

Stay current on technology. The age of technology and information is here to serve you.

They can't step on you if you don't lie down.

Understand what lifestyle you want. All your decisions should be in harmony with that choice.

Vote. If you don't vote, you have no right to complain.

Write in a journal on a consistent basis.

X-hibit good taste in all you do and say.

❦

You can create a dramatic entrance when you enter a room by pausing, and then walking into the room confidently.

❦

Zealously do what is practical, but live as if anything is possible.

Author's Notes

The ABC's of Life book was my first published book back in 1994. Many things have changed in the book business since then, but I still remember getting this book out into the world.

Since it was before the internet, I had to go to the library to find the addresses of publishers and agents so I could send them a query letter.

I can't remember how many letters I sent, but I remember I had a fairly large collection of rejection letters. However, a small publisher eventually called me and said he would publish the book because his mother loved the book. I was thrilled and thankful for his mother, who believed girls needed my written advice.

If you shopped at bookstores in the mid-'90s, then you might have seen this book by the cash register at places like Barnes and Noble or perhaps heard me on one of those radio stations that used to interview authors.

One of my favorite memories was when a woman at the gym showed me this book she had purchased, and the author had the same name as me. I don't remember which of us was more astonished.

Later my publisher, with the gracious mother, decided to publish only travel books and returned the book rights to me. And although a second publisher asked for permission to print it himself in his country, which I granted, it's been me as the publisher ever since.

Have I kept my own advice? Mostly. I'm still a work in progress, but I don't learn the hard way as much as I used to.

I've updated this book a few times but haven't changed it as much as one might think. Although times have changed since 1994, I believe the advice is basically sound, and I know people have enough wisdom to choose what works for them and leave the rest.

I hope that everything I write helps to expand the reader's world to include more possibilities and fewer mistakes and that this book has been part of that process for you. —Beca

Facebook: https://www.facebook.com/becalewiscreative
Facebook: https://www.facebook.com/becalewisfans
Instagram: https://instagram.com/becalewis
TikTok: https://tiktok.com/@becalewis
Twitter: http://twitter.com/becalewis
LinkedIn: https://linkedin.com/in/becalewis
Youtube: https://www.youtube.com/c/becalewis

Also By Beca

The Ruby Sisters Series: Women's Lit, Friendship
A Last Gift, After All This Time,
The Karass Chronicles: Magical Realism, Friendship
Karass, Pragma, Jatismar, Exousia, Stemma, Paragnosis
Karass Chronicles Novels: Magical Realism, Friendship
In-Between, Missing, Out Of Nowhere
The Return To Erda Series: Fantasy
Shatterskin, Deadsweep, Abbadon, The Experiment
The Chronicles of Thamon: Fantasy
Banished, Betrayed, Discovered, Wren's Story
The Shift Series: Spiritual Self-Help
Living in Grace: The Shift to Spiritual Perception
The Daily Shift: Daily Lessons From Love To Money
The 4 Essential Questions: Choosing Spiritually Healthy Habits
The 28 Day Shift To Wealth: A Daily Prosperity Plan
The Intent Course: Say Yes To What Moves You

Imagination Mastery: A Workbook For Shifting Your Reality
Right Thinking: A Thoughtful System for Healing
Perception Mastery: Seven Steps To Lasting Change
Perception Parables: Very short stories
Love's Silent Sweet Secret: A Fable About Love
Golden Chains And Silver Cords: A Fable About Letting Go

Advice:
A Woman's ABC's of Life: Lessons in Love, Life, and Career from Those Who Learned The Hard Way

About Beca

Beca writes books she hopes will change people's perceptions of themselves and the world, and open possibilities to things and ideas that are waiting to be seen and experienced.

At sixteen, Beca founded her own dance studio. Later, she received a Master's Degree in Dance in Choreography from UCLA and founded the Harbinger Dance Theatre, a multimedia dance company, while continuing to run her dance school.

After graduating—to better support her three children—Beca switched to the sales field, where she worked as an employee and independent contractor to many industries, excelling in each while perfecting and teaching her Shift® system, and writing books.

She joined the financial industry in 1983 and became an Associate Vice President of Investments at a major stock brokerage firm, and was a licensed Certified Financial Planner for over twenty years.

This diversity, along with a variety of life challenges, helped fuel the desire to share what she's learned by writing and speaking, hoping it will make a difference in other people's lives.

Beca grew up in State College, PA, with the dream of becoming a dancer and then a writer. She carried that dream forward as she fulfilled a childhood wish by moving to Southern California in 1968. Beca told her family she would never move back to the cold.

After living there for thirty-one years, she met her husband Delbert Lee Piper, Sr., at a retreat in Virginia, and everything changed. They decided to find a place they could call their own, which sent them off traveling around the United States. They lived and worked in a few different places before returning to live in the cold once again near Del's family in a small town in Northeast Ohio, not too far from State College.

When not working and teaching together, they love to visit and play with their combined family of eight children and five grandchildren, read, study, do yoga or taiji, feed birds, and work in their garden.

www.ingramcontent.com/pod-product-compliance
Lightning Source LLC
Chambersburg PA
CBHW072055290426
44110CB00014B/1690